Thistle

Mx. Yaffa

All rights reserved.

Published in 2025 by Meraj Publishing
1st Edition

Illustrations copyright © 2025
This is a work of creative nonfiction & poetry. It reflects the author's present recollections of experiences over time. Some parts or names have been fictionalized in varying degrees, for various purposes.

No part of this book may be reproduced or used in any manner without written permission of the copyright owner except for the use of quotations in a book review. For more information, address: **info@merajpublishing.com**

ISBN: 979-8-9925727-7-3 (Print)
ISBN: 979-8-9925727-8-0 (Ebook)

Cover by Mishandi Sarhan

merajpublishing.com

To the caretakers; the family members, lovers, strangers.
To those who stitch our pieces back together through care.
May we remember we are never whole without care.

Other Titles by Yaffa:

Blood Orange
Desecrated Poppies
Inara
Sage
Whispers Beneath the Orange Grove
Living to 99
Letters From a Living Utopia

Original Foreword Written March 7, 2023 9
It Ends 13
    We Were 14
    They Say 15
    Best Friend 16
    OG 17
    Privilege 18
    I Know 20
    Come Back 21
The Beginning 23
    Hope 24
    Agony 26
    Home 27
    On the Horizon 28
    A Poet 29
    Rare 30
    1 in 5 31
    In the Park 32
    Kids 33
    3AM 34
    With the World 35
    Endless 36
    On the Ground 37
    Everywhere 39
    To Do List 40
    Death Merchant 41
    G 43
    Leaving 44
    Tears 46
    Spiral 47

Beyond	48
Wood	49
Ex	50
Last March	51
Beyond Words	53
Okay	54
Testament	55
Leukemia	56
Rupture	57
Tired	58
Spirits	60
It Is	61
Begging	64
I Want	65
Years From Now	67
Lifetime of Estrangement	69
Ghosts	70
Sand	74
The Last Time	77
Goose	78
Clinical	80
Evelyn	81
Waiting	83
Worker Bees	84
Code Grey	85
Oblivion	86
Thanksgiving	87
Family Without Blood	89
White Tears	90
Back	92

Settlers	93
7 Sisters	94
Sunday	95
Not Family	97
Accountability	99
Mala for Healing	100
2-3 Lessons	101
Punishing Health	102
Love	103
PTSD	104
Care and Love	106
Growth	107
Weinkom (Where Are You?)	108
Death Threats	110
In Reverse	112
I am	116
So Close So far	119
Mourn	120
Mala for Caretaking	121
Panic Attacks	122
200	123
Bends and Always Breaks	124
What Is and What Will Be	125
Again	128
Beyond	129
The Girl	130
Guests	132
Yawn	134
Cry	135
Epilogue	137

Acknowledgements.. 140
About Yaffa..141
About Meraj Publishing.. 141

If you'd like to listen to this book in audio form, please scan the QR code for access below:

Original Foreword Written March 7, 2023

As a poet, I dream, unknowingly layering words in endless languages, building utopia with every letter.

I used to think I was only a novelist. Fantasy and creative nonfiction had poured out of me since I was 13. Now, I know better. I am a poet who sometimes writes poetic novels.

I wrote my first poem in this collection while sitting beside my sister during her most intense round of chemotherapy. It was her third out of a potential four rounds. The first two rounds resulted in ICU visits, but I wasn't there.

That January, living in Belfast, I knew something was wrong. It took me a few days to be able to name that she was not okay after round one. Sleep abandoned me for days, and as I stared at the full moon one night, I knew. I called my other sister and asked if she knew. She said she had posted on Facebook but had not heard from her. My sister contacted me a few days later, after leaving the ICU.

She asked me to come for round three. I flew over, quarantining in this COVID world, to be there - again.

Sitting by her side transported me back to when I was 17. I had watched loved ones die while chemo poured into their veins.

I saw everyone I loved dying then, as I did for years after 17.

I remained frozen in March 2021 for nearly two years.

The cancer cleared after that third round. A victory most of us did not expect.

Then, in June 2022, as I was about to visit her without the weight of cancer between us for the first time in years, the call came - it had metastasized. No chemo this time, only excruciating pain and surgery.

The floodgates opened, and these poems came through me, in this exact order, these exact words. Only the spelling has been modified. Nothing else.

This is the story of watching a loved one survive and die at the same time. It is not about my sister or me, or either of our outcomes. It is about witnessing.

I wrote this for the global majority - Trans, Muslim, disabled, and displaced Indigenous Folks who are not permitted to witness our loved ones. Instead, we are relegated to voices of our identities, as if we do not witness and experience our own cancer and death due to terminal illness. Or as if we do not love and that death is not a constant in our relationships.

These poems are love for every person whose story is erased in the guise of representing single identities.

This is for me, you, and everyone.

2025 Update

Three years have past since I sat in spaces that I now occupy to write these words. Much has changed as you can imagine. Three years is potentially multiple lifetimes for Stage 4 Cancer. Three years is potentially multiple lifetimes around family. Three years are multiple lifetimes in a world where genocide feeds off our family lines and sells us products in return.

These poems are still largely unaltered, but I have also added a few poems to the beginning before the original poetry written more recently. My sister died July, 2025. She is home, and these words can now find their own home.

It Ends

July 2025

We Were

I will not sugarcoat
our relationship
now that you've gone

we were messy
we were loving
we were family

you were not a saint
I am not a saint

in between conflict,
growth,
care,
we lived

may you finally
finally
rest

They Say

she's nearing the end now.
she'd be in hospice if she wasn't too fragile to be released from hospital.
and all the stuff we thought might be problems have turned into problems.

Best Friend

I told my best
friend that you're
dying
she didn't know
who you were

no one currently
in my life
knew you
not even your
ghost

as if you
were never
really here

why is it
everyone I mourn
feels like a
hallucination?

no one there
to validate
that they even
existed, let alone
that I loved

I'm tired
of mourning people
no one
will ever know
about

OG

you were the
original poetry

                              even that's moved
                                        on

Privilege

she's frail
bones jutting out
in angles as sharp
as my sorrow

I see myself
at 17, the weight of
a revolution that
isn't mine
on my heart
the cold bench
my only source
of warmth

you go in and out
I go wherever it is
broken hearted
souls go
I missed you
or maybe I
missed the you
I never knew
the one that
lived in my mind
whose death I feared
whose communication I
resented

was I
so desperate for
a sister that
I gave up
my soul?

your chest rises

and falls and I wonder
if maybe it is
time
I yearn for time
but I do not have the privilege
to witness a loved one
die

you will die
I have already
grieved
others will die
the same day
I will grieve them
instead

I Know

I wake up

refuse to acknowledge
why

I know you've
died

you don't quite
come to me
to say it

but you barely said
it alive

I know
my body begs
to stay awake
do something
with the knowledge

I slip back to sleep
message waiting
for me when I
wake

Come Back

you died
no friend of mine
even knew you

I wonder if
I should text your
mom

I wonder if
I should tell my
mom

I wonder if
anyone I know
would care

I wonder if
I'm even allowed
to care

it doesn't feel
real

I've mourned
you a thousand
times
across 100
communities
you have always
come back

.... come back
...

but also don't

please rest

let us all
rest, now

The Beginning

March 2021

Hope

latex gloves and gowns
welcome me to my
sister's room

she lays motionless
speaking softly and
welcoming the chemo
and I,

ask how
she is and

she
mutters "tired, "exhausted"
from a night of
continuous bathroom
breaks and shattering
alarms anytime she
moves

the food network plays
inviting sounds and flavors
of culture and food
of tournaments of champions
and diners, Guy Fieri is
welcome here, and he is always
here

I drown out the buzzing
and the sounds and we
talk and laugh, shielding
us both from the lowered
heart rate and treatment
delays, and they swoop in
like kind vultures knowing

Death is near and I'm too far
behind

I see it with my eyes, she
feels it with her everything
and we both know, and I
smile another joke, and she
laughs as I text crying
emojis beyond these
four walls where
death rules and pot
is not allowed

I drive to a house
that is not mine
drink citrus tea and
cry myself to sleep
to do it all over again
the day before, the day
after, hoping, praying
loving, and letting go

June 2022

Agony

during the day
we laugh
between appointments and errands
conversations to transform
our lives

during the night
the house weeps In agony
every step breaking
creaking shattering
our souls

Home

I was not expecting
to find home between cancer
and your embrace
your smile
your grace
your invitation for
the family that I am
lost, yearning, searching
I always wanted closeness
with family
now I know that
it is you (here)

On the Horizon

I stand
one suitcase
one bag
grounded (by your need for me)
the aircrew said
we had to land
due to turbulence
and cancer
metastasizing
where it never should be

I am here now
grounded (by your need for me)
forever
always
on the horizon
waiting for the next flight

A Poet

I am not
a poet
an essayist and novelist
maybe
but I think of you and
poetry flows
like a well
that never believed
in its own existence

Rare

they say
it's rare
for a tumor
like this
to pop up
where it has
as if there has never been
and never will be
another

it's true
there will never be
another you

<u>1 in 5</u>

I heard you
say on a call
that there are only
4 or so, other
cases like
yours

1 in 5
make it

am I selfish
to want
you to be
the 1 in 5

?

In the Park

F and I are in the park
and I wonder who
will take him
home,
after

I wonder
if it can be
me

a siren goes off
in the distance
he stirs,
whimpers

I put my forehead
to his, not sure if
I'm comforting him or
myself

telling him
and me
she'll be okay

it's only then
that I realize
maybe
they're here for
you

Kids

you won't meet
my kids
partners
or the me
of tomorrow

I won't meet
your kids
like I met
your partners
your soul
your being

3AM

I wake up
in the middle
of the night

to write a
few words
here and there

fearful
I may lose them
like I'm losing you

With the World

I want to
publish these
words

am I a
bad person
for wanting to

share you
with the
world

?

Endless

I love
You

You
Are endless

I honor
You

You
Are endless

I miss
You

You
Are endless

I hold
You

You
Are endless

You are
Endless
Endless
Endless

On the Ground

you're lying
on the ground
groaning in
pain

I'm on
my laptop
drafting a work
document

I hear you
I shiver
I don't do or say
anything

you're dying
in front
of me
again

nothing I can
do, but be
here, there, and
everywhere

thoughts and voices
creep from every
direction, telling me

I should do more
pick you up
hug you
everything

but I'm here

alone, watching
waiting for things to get
better

your screams
echo in
response

Everywhere

we talk
about magic, past lives
spirits and guides
and ghosts that
demand more
than is welcome

I tell you
about the fire
the loss of everything
and there's understanding
in your closed eyes

learn and move on
you say, and I know
I will, that I can
gratitude and movement
no loss anchoring
me like a prisoner

chainless, floating
finding you between space
and time, with
every crow, every plant
everything that is you and
that is me, everywhere

To Do List

Smoothie
Chai
Bananas royale from Baskin robins,
strawberry cheesecake and something with almonds/nuts
rocky road caramel bananas
cherries almonds
Purple purse we both like
Colostomy

Lifestyle/sex collar in San Francisco
Do research over ice cream
Walnut creek for harps/lane Bryant
Plan trip together (sooner rather than later) fall
Diner
Dumplings
Star chart

Death Merchant

your screams echo

I leave the bath
early, so your pain
slowly fades

you say, I might
*have to ask you
to stay, I lie*
say i don't mind

I don't know if
I mind, or if i do
not, wonder
if I will ever know

i lie in bed
wondering about
how for a long
long time, i

was a death merchant
one of the best
leaving death
everywhere i went

now i lie here
in bed
asking for dreams
tonight

begging the universe
that this time I leave death
behind

I have lost count
of all those I have supported
in death,
a death merchant
a death doula
even a birthing doula

I have claimed
life and death
yet here I struggle to
claim either
do i, or
you would know
how to help me
but I do not
want that word near
you, ever again

G

G and I
are friends
she is yours
and I am yours
but maybe, just
maybe, we also exist
outside of
you

I think you
want us to
live outside of
you

she reminded me
that constant death
makes it normal
and makes us
more sensitive to
death
it makes me
more sensitive to
death

she reminded me
to seek support
help that I may need
we will be here
a while and

I wonder if I'll
ever lose myself
enough to want you
gone

Leaving

driving away
yesterday, you asked
h*ow I felt about
you dying.* It felt
like I lied, but I
am not sure.
I said, *it is hard,
but I have closure.
I celebrate every
moment.
death does not
destroy me
anymore*

there are 28
pages of
poems here
saying otherwise
maybe they are
both true

death is beautiful
the journey is hard
I will miss you
in this state
and I will be happy
for you, here and
when you are home

sometimes, it feels
like my pain is
just for others
to feed
off

like, I can't
say I'm happy
today, or any
of these days

then I am a
bad sibling
and I do not
care about you

I care, but I will
not selfishly take
your pain as
my own

you are you
I am me
we intersect in
every life
and we meet
again

we will meet again

Tears

there are
unshed tears
on this street
and I wonder
where they will find
home, if my home
is on this street too

Spiral

                    you tell me
                    you're spiraling
                    I do not say
                    I am too
                    I felt it
                    I felt you
                    and my blood
                    boiled, my breath
                    weakened
                    my bones yearned
                    for comfort
                    anxiety not my
                    own, yours
                    I feel you
                    everywhere
                    you tell me
                    things through
                    my blood, my bones
                    my being, your being

                                                      I spiral too

Beyond

you say
I am beyond
boundaries, because
I feel like a part
of you?

you place the
question mark
leaving the
universe to
answer our
familial bond
beyond blood
beyond choice
just is

I remind you, or
I say
that you are
the priestess
beyond time and space
they are yours
and you deserve
a break
beyond

Wood

wood cries
sizzling in a
fire of my own
making

it sounds
like you

bones breaking
from within
a fire burning
throughout

like the fire
you beg for it to stop

like the wood
the fire in
your bones
rages

until,
there's nothing left

Ex

I am
with my ex
camping in
the catskills
high and talking
about all that
could have been

he doesn't say
it
but he asks why
I am the one to be
there, with you

he doesn't say
that maybe things
would be different
if I had not watched
you dying
last year
and throughout

I wonder what
could have been
knowing I'd be there
either way

Last March

it was last
March
as i sat by
your side
in a hospital
room like so many
others

I left him
in tears
the day I
flew to you

I was meant
to quarantine for
days but you
called and asked
if I'd come anyways

"you're safe"
you said, and I convinced
you to wait
anyways

a negative test
later, I was by
your side, watching
you fall in and out
of sleep, wondering
if I'd know if
something wasn't
right

I smiled
I joked

I pretended
that he
did not die
in a hospital
room, like so
many others
with the same
fluids

going back
I knew nothing
could be the
same

I tried
anyways
I always
try anyways

we said goodbye
near the day
I booked my
flight
a year older
a year heavier
a lifetime wiser
endlessly grateful

Beyond Words

I do not
want words

not for who I am
or what we are

I want to exist
beyond words

where being is
all there is
outside of
labels and expectations
I am limitless

I am beyond
words

Okay

I ask my body
why we were
dissociative
knowing that we will be
fine

that's the fear
it responded
not that we
worry that we will
not be okay
that we will be

that your death
will not throw our life
off the universal
rails

that we will be
okay
and what that says
about us

as if saying
letting go means
we never cared
at all

Testament

as I received
a Korean body
scrub, I reminded my
bodymind that
being ok when
it happens
is a testament
to growth
to your love
and my love
and to the reality
that losing you
has already thrown
me off the universal
rails

I have been angry,
in denial,
desperately clinging,
and finally letting
go

I have mourned you
and when you die
I will be ok
and I know it
makes it easier for you
to let go too

Leukemia

I'm yelling and screaming
kicking and thrashing
searching for a girl
whose mom is dying from leukemia
and she's disappeared and no one
seems to care

I'm back in the guest
bedroom
dreaming and sweating
in the Berkley cold
dreaming of cancer and loss
I'd do it anyway
to find you

Rupture

I hear you groaning
under the weight of fentanyl and oxy
a tumor rupturing you
from your office
a few feet and a world away

f rushes to you
looks at me
do something
he says
lying by you
glaring at me
as I

i...i
eat a melted sundae
texting on tinder
watching tv

                                          anything to look away

Tired

I try
reading No Shade
in Aztlan
lounging in the
UCSF ground floor
lounge in the adult
hospital
the leather creases
under my 165lb
frame and I sit back
in a white dress
with purple flowers
and I am too tired
to read about the
heat and yearnings of
anyone else

I nearly fall
asleep
six hours in
between working
labs, ct scans, and
endless stuffed animal shopping

I am tired
brain shutting down
somersaulting
Nov 1st
the day I am meant
to go to
Hawaii
the day of your
surgery

and my brain is stuck on a

plane
trying to balance
me, her, them
free falling into
oblivion

free falling into
sleep

Spirits

I feel her
calling out
I don't know who she is
or why she calls
to me

she calls me in
my dreams
she wakes me
and I feel her
right outside

she is not you
she is long passed

you say Spirits
do not enter
your home

I know
they linger
outside
as if waiting

hungry
for one of us to join
them

It Is

it's the hummingbird
ruby throated mating call
swooping in and out of view
the female hovering gracefully
by the yellow flowers before
meeting him in the tree
for some private time

it's F jerking his leg away
dremel tearing away
fis overgrown nails
ticklish but never laughing
the glaring he gives us
for a bath he never asked for

it's the noticing a tiger
jacket in a store for hours
knowing that the attendant
means well, throws microaggression
after microaggression
and we both wonder where the line
between micro and macro is
I say *I'm used to it*
you say *we shouldn't have to be*
both of us saying what the other
already knows

it's the fashion show at
outback, where Venus meets the west
where most styles are appropriated
but the sales people are kind
know you by name
stay two hours after closing
one day, two days because
they care

it's the conversation about
accessibility and small businesses
and chains
judgment for Starbucks
when it's the only one
you can order on your phone
told you're ruining the world
shut up and stay home
they say
if we get rid of store chains
what then?
I say back - yearning
for others to build Utopia with

it's B's dinner parties
the ones you're too tired for
but host anyways

it's the casual conversation
the saying I hate Canada
trashing neoliberal institutions
named after royalty and what not
it's the mispronouncing my name
as I forget theirs

it's the stone room
the other stone room
the anklets and bracelets
the onyx crow
the hummingbirds waiting
to be bought
the hundreds of dollars of rings
made of Karen silver
finally a benefit to
terrorists
as Beyonce would call them
as China would classify

Tibetan owners
stones that heal
call to me and you

it's the bonding
the time we would not
spend together if you weren't
dying
the tears we would
spend apart
like a
who I haven't talked to
since March this cold
October night

it's the rose quartz
i'm gifting every sister
it's the love
the pain
the laughter
the growth
talking about nudity
and sex and living

it's the living
you and I
F and B
eight other sisters
mostly you and I

Begging

it's bad tonight
your screams hovering
all around me
tightly embracing my soul
begging for a reaction
there is none
my body shakes
aches from your pain

I feel my body
shutting down
disassociating
so I write
trying to figure out
how I can
show up for you
do I delay my flight?
do I cancel?

what happens if
I'm not here?
how do I live
my life knowing
you might not be here
when I land?

I Want

it was a bad night
a very sick day
now asleep

I wonder if
I'll actually
leave tomorrow

I usually know
these things
whether I leave or not

this time
just feels...
exhausting

I want to stay
I want to leave
I want....

I want cancer
to
not exist

I want medicine
to
react quicker

I want you
to
have joy

every day
every moment
everywhere

and I know
you already are
you do joy

you are joy
and I witness
share and amplify
it all

Years From Now

years from now,
they'll ask me
at a writing event
if you read these poems
about you

years from now,
I'd say that publishing
takes time
unsure where you
are

years from now,
I'd say that
you didn't read them
you lived through and
with them

years from now,
I'll remember the smiles,
the difficult conversations,
the thriving
and

years from now,
I'll still be scared
to lose you too soon
knowing you'll always
be here

years from now,
writing about you
staying alive will still be
harder than writing about
you dying

years from now,
I will love you
endlessly
forever
always

Lifetime of Estrangement

I think
I am tired
bone deep ache

I pretend
it's from my flight
across Oceans

I know
it is an abyss of pain
a lifetime of estrangement

I Googled
the antonym
of belonging

I needed
a word for
my pain

I desire
to understand why
it is

I recognize
it is beyond
me

I am not tired
due to a 14 hour
flight or due to meaningless
work or jet lag

I am tired
I am tired   I am tired

Ghosts

I'm reading
cemetery boys
you rush past
not seeing me
as if I'm a ghost
groaning in Pain
towards a bath that
muffles your cries
I sit here
F on his bed
listening to Ahwak
and lil Nas x
reading about ghosts
like me

your screams echo

Nina Simone is on
now, I Wait
trying to read
knowing I can't
so I write
typing away
knowing I'm not okay
and not knowing how to not
be, I wonder
if this is a hospital
pain, the one prophesied
by my arrival

I remember N
telling me to slow down
as we went 25 miles an hour
on a blizzard covered highway
after his stroke

at 3AM
I still woke up for
work, like nothing had
happened, and in my dissociation
nothing did
we took a drive
I blocked out doctors
outing him in front of
me, but I honored him
by not hearing a word
until he told me
years later
in a hot tub we couldn't
be naked in anymore

I listen to W Btir
aching to gift the song
to someone, anyone
who won't take it too
seriously, but will fly under
every note, every star
lifted by the grace of
my love

I yearn to matter
knowing that I matter
but I am not God
I yearn to be
a God that can stop
the pain, stop the cycles
the downpouring in
the Carolinas
that can reverse climate change
save Puerto Rico
save you
save me

I yearn to fly

away, into
oblivion and beyond

you asked me
why I'm drawn to pain?
how do I tell you
that you are pain
you are what I grieve
in this and every
life

I am not drawn to
pain
I am drawn to
you
I am drawn to your
love
I am not drawn to your
death
I am drawn to your
endlessness
I am drawn to my
endlessness

you walk out
seven songs later
2 coke cans
in your hands
you walk to your
chair, as if I'm
not here
maybe you know
what I haven't learned

I'm not really here
I am a haunting
a spirit holding onto
lives that are no longer

mine

you say the pain is
a 9
B says
that's never happened
I say
I know

you ask if I know
how to
administer narcan
I say I do
I don't - it has been too long
years since the last time
I needed the skill
but I know how
to Google
to remember

I'm ready
waiting
I am here

                      I go to work

Sand

I do not
go back and forth
trying to fix
these perfect words

in poetry I am
free to explore
to decolonize and tear
apart language that
was never mine

there is no
respecting the grammar
the artform of
the white cises who
have come before
leaving a footprint
in the sand that
left no sand

that told people
like me there
was never any
sand that
we needed to pay
for sand through blood
and workshops

years of editing
to be told that
we are now taking
up all the sand
it is not fair
they say
The Sand should

be shared
they say

gaslighting us
into believing we
hoarded the sand
thousands of
miles away from
the beach
having only heard
of this sand

my poetry is
perfect
but it does not
take away my hatred
for this sand
the worst part
of the beach is
the sand
your sand
finding its way
into every crevice
holding onto
my hair for
weeks

I love the beach
you may keep
your sand
that you deny ever
existed that
you say I stole
from you and
hid in my gorgeous
scalp

I and my scalp
will take the water
water without sand
is a miracle
sand without water
is a nuisance
you are a nuisance
and
my poetry is
perfect

The Last Time

this feels
like the last time
I'll be here

I've felt this before
time and again
and I return
renewed hope

waiting
not sure
what for
for me or
for them
to show up
differently

home is where
death lives
misery
anger
none in good
ways

this will
not be
the last time

Goose

I wiped a golden
goose egg that
replaced your anus
in a way
that i did not
know anuses could
be transformed into
it was clinical
and I wonder if
in a different life
I could be a doctor
outside of a medical
system built to
kill and entrap us

it is strange
watching someone
helped by this system
without causing more
harm

strange that your pain
is less and you feel
better, for I
have only experienced
doctors as trying to kill me
only to be revived by other
doctors
as if to say that they are
the medical gods
they take life and
give it back
it is ours
if you agree we may
save you

I sit here
listening to you
on a disability access
call for this same
hospital that forced you
to fight every day
and I know that if it were
my brownness and transness
where you lay
I would be long gone

Clinical

I dab and dab
and dab
iodine layering
your skin
the golden goose
does not pop
or retreat

I am
a clinician
every movement
clinical and sterile

i am not here
concentrating on
the task
trying to
revive your
dead skin from
a dead soul

***
Brown 12. 8

Blood 10. 5
5
***

Evelyn

she screams
help
listen to me
please
I'll tell you everything
the EMS says they found
her at the park
walking into traffic
saying the same things
she said *awww* when she sat
thinks maybe she was assaulted
as 7 large male
EMTs Cops and doctors surround her
on a wheelchair she tries
to break out of

they don't know her name
a white nurse claims it's
Evelyn
she comes a lot she says
the 6' 5" emt says it's not Evelyn
their whiteness argues over
the blackness of the person
thrashing
a white doctor comes with half
a dozen needles
tells her *she needs medicine*
first time any doctor has talked
to her

they scream, genderless outside
of assumptions
the males hold them
down
they yell for help

wheeled away after

five minutes later
the screams are drowned
by the smiles of workers
groans of other patients
welcome to UCSF
maybe Evelyn

5 hours later
Evelyn screams
unseen, un heard

Waiting

S sleeps
not really
lies maybe?
on a gurney
that I requested
as they stared
in disbelief
...
I am tired
we slide from one
side of the room
to the next
two hours in
waiting

the nurse gives me
a chair
the one who medicated
Evelyn
the first nurse telling me
I had to stand

I ache
feel that I'm
being unfair

they help
don't they?
so why does it
feel like death?

Worker Bees

I watch them
dozens of them
buzzing like bees
between the beds lining
the halls, the machines
the advocacy offices in the crevices

some smile
some look stressed
the speakers are blaring
code grey ...
again and again

they
are
not
fully
to
blame
when they have inches of space

to save

Code Grey

ice chips
blankets
anything to let
your veins rise
to where they can
access
them
code grey
code grey
only twice this time

I think about
existence
watching the world
unfolding
everything will
and won't
I see beyond
the building
beyond San Francisco
beyond existence
everything flows
everything is
I am at peace
between the screams
the pain, the death
it is

I am

Oblivion

I write
I release
every word
no longer living
inside me
no longer requiring
validation and action
I float away
into peace and Oblivion
lighter still
writing from above

Thanksgiving

I don't feel
honored
I say
the anniversary
of the massacre of
Indigenous people
is a time of Mourning
a trigger caused by the
white and brown
folks who celebrate
genocide behind concepts
of gratitude and friendships
I say *I do not*
want your gratitude or friendship
if it means the continued
spillage of our blood and genocide
you lie in a hospital bed
you ask *where I will go*
we both know I won't
go anywhere until
you have care lined up
that I asked for in September

you have lined up
all care, except on the one day
I say *it feels like my wrists*
are bleeding, my throat thrashing
my heart stabbed and pierced with
shots of bronze and steel
I yearn for the hills and the sea
the olives and oranges spilled
bleeding red in harvest

I do not feel honored

your whiteness careless
with my indigeneity in a land
that is neither of ours
but I have no home
to die in
so I bleed
feel the land bleed
everywhere
everything
no honor
only death

I begged for a
single day in exchange
for a lifetime of
care
you reminded me
we are not the same
only one of us comes from
genocide, the other
enacts it

Family Without Blood

your 38 years of cancer
outweigh my 30 years of trauma
but they do not outweigh the decades
of displacement And ancestral trauma
I carry with me everyday

trauma I mourn this week and every day
trauma your people celebrate this very week
and benefit off of every day

I needed space.   to honor my people
and you did nothing to honor me
we have said *we are family, without blood*

now,
I wonder if we are anything at all

White Tears

you cry
all i see are white tears
taking up space
you say you're sorry
about this week
as if I hadn't asked
dozens of times
to have one day
away
one day to step
away from you and
yours, settlers
not on their way
home

one day to honor
my own peoples
genocides
as i stay here
on stolen land
stolen by your
people, now I'm here
caring for you
instead
one day
wasn't granted
months of caretaking
a sister lost

am I wrong? for being hurt?
for asking for one thing
or am I wrong for a part of me thinking
you were not capable of supporting me
which is worse? Believing or hopelessness
if you die -My anxiety always goes there

will the answer change?
will I hate myself then?

why is it that I only ever hate myself
around my sisters?

Back

back at the hospital
lying on the seats
waiting for results
I'm not sure if I want you to be admitted
or to be home
home's been hard, for you
this week's been hard for me
I wonder if these next few weeks
will in fact be
the last
for my presence
as a caretaker/sibling

Settlers

seething with anger and hiding in my room
like a teenager
watching a show I'm embarrassed of

I shall hide here forever
asked for one thing,
told *it's not
possible*, now the neighbors are coming over for dinner
she says
"oh it's okay they hate it like us"
I needed a day
to honor people
genocided
now, she invites white
settlers for a dinner
I change her bandages
anyways, I sit in silence
anyways

someone offers
"do you need a rescue mission rn?
I could swoop you up
take you somewhere for at least a little while"
but i stay here
in a room
in a house
I no longer feel safe in

7 Sisters

I lost
7 sisters
this year
I am not sure
where I left them

1 has been missing for years
5 hurt my soul and
1 hurt me the most

I yearn to
miss them
but alas
they were never there
to be missed

they took and
took and took
until there was nothing
left

then, I gave
and gave and gave
willingly and unwillingly
from the ends of my life
and they took

now they are gone
and I have reserves and savings
space to begin a life
whenever - wherever

Sunday

on a Sunday morning
two days after
Indigenous day of Mourning
I realized I was tired of feeling hurt
by my family, the sisters that claim me
as a brother
not realizing I am but a ghost
they violently hurt
from time to time

on a Sunday morning
I facilitated a conversation
with other queer
and trans Muslims
about settler colonialism and
settlerhood and our positionality
here, on this land
where we never belong
where the violence from whites never
ends, even from within our families

on a Sunday afternoon
I knew that I had not mourned
at all, I had not connected
only disconnected because
whiteness demanded to be centered
as always

on a Sunday evening
I grew tired from managing white people's emotions and
their need to be comforted
after enacting violence
I have held onto pain
my entire life

this Sunday I realize
I have been holding onto
sisters, gone now

I am beyond
pain

Not Family

I don't want to call you my sisters
for sisters are meant to cut you
and reopen your wounds for all time
never showing up in the smallest of ways
not even to manipulate you to show up more
when you already show up Endlessly

you have been more considerate already
than all the sisters combined
you asked for my pronouns
the name to use
perhaps it's because I am more
of a parent
who abandoned you years ago
that you treat me well, enough

I can not call you my children
not in a World that does not recognize
sibling labor as true or
I'm not sure who I am to you or
who you are to me
family is synonymous with pain
we are not family

I had nine sisters at one point
I forget that I died
I have none in this life
I miss them at Fajr
like I miss
my children that I birthed
in previous lives

you came at Fajr
the visual
an inversion of a womb

pulling me into you
leaving nothing behind
only sisters can make me
want to die
I want to die

Accountability

one conversation
two
and we begin healing
my cancer moon
can hold a grudge
like no one's business
while cancer kills you
but I carry so many pains
a single apology is enough
to release what I carry
I move on
filled with your
accountability

Mala for Healing

quartz amethyst lapis aquamarine calcite carnelian red jasper crystal and smokey quartz in hearts

quartz chevron azurite malachite turquoise natural citrine red tigers eye dalmation jasper

quartz fluorite angelite aquamarine golden tigers eye carnelian smokey quartz

quartz fluorite lapis amazonite yellow adventurine red tigers eye black onyx

quartz aura 23 amethyst aquamarine rose quartz citrine carnelian black tourmaline crystal praise and Baltic amber

Tara blessing

2-3 Lessons

talking to V
I share I have grown
immensely

the number 1
which is actually 2 or 3
is recognizing that I am
community

number 1
maybe 2
I let go of the concept
of sisterhood
and using it as an excuse
to not live my life
2 years ago
Seedo dying
reminded me to build
for me
how quickly I forgot

3 or maybe 1 or 2
I want to find growth
not wait for it
to find me
between trauma and pain

forgetting is healing
it is not abandonment

Punishing Health

I mourn a home
that pretended to love
but told me I expired
at the end of a visa

Love

white people saw us claiming things
thought they could do the same
not realizing that we claim from love
and claiming is sharing and gifting,
not taking.

PTSD

you say
*the sound of voices
after helium is now
triggering
your body pushing you
into a panic attack*
you say *it's irrational
this anger you have
at people doing this
to themselves when...*
when you had it done to
you, when it can still happen
trying to process the ER
Evelyn, them calling you
a name not your own
recognizing that maybe
this is rooted in childhood
when they took you away
as a two year old and
you can't remember
you ask me to talk through it
with you, apologizing for waking
me up
we both know the universe
woke me in anticipation
for this
I am here
I feel light
this, peer support,
I know how to do
to not carry your things
to bring in bits and pieces of
my journey as we walk
as I stare in wonder at you

you are magic
your brain believes it
it would not have invited
you to this otherwise

Care and Love

I write less
as pain slowly
trickles away
as trauma leaves
this house and
my neck flexes
moves freely, my
body no longer
breaking under
the weight of
care and love
no, not care and love
inequitable responsibility
and forced roles
care and love lift
I am lifted now

Growth

I want
growth in 2023
but not growth from
pain and trauma
the growth that I nearly
die through

I want growth that
I seek in the midst
of community
bathed in belonging and
inspiration
growth, growth, growth?

whiteness took learning
away from me at 9
replaced with survival

19 years later
I am ready

Weinkom (Where Are You?)

writing a report
to send to yt
people who can not
understand it
I realize that I hold
anger, so much anger
towards my family
all of them, S, D, E,
L, A, mama and
Baba, just not
the babies

where were they?
when the pills found
my belly and didn't
let go for 40ish
hours

where were they?
when three hospitals
tossed me around
like an expired salad
burying the mold
no one wants

where were they?
when I was so cold
sleeping on a bench
dodging men trying
to rape me
my stomach empty
except for the air
I desperately wanted
to deny it

where were they?
after every breakup
after the dozens of losses

where are they now?
when we haven't
properly talked in
months, years even

in 40 houses
13 years, and 10
countries
no sister has ever visited
a home of mine
perhaps if they do
it'd no longer be home

Death Threats

I did not leave
social media because
of the death threats
although, that's what
I tell folks
I felt validated by them
I left because
I looked around
there was no one left
only ghosts of others
holding onto ghosts of me
ghosts they felt were
everything that I am
frozen in time
where growth was never
possible, where they never
had to pick up the phone
because they knew
I was still alive
and alive is
all that ever mattered
to ghosts who also
cry themselves to sleep
and don't know whether
they'll be alive in
the mourning
who die every day
as I die every day
in a monotonous
cycle of death and
ghosts

I left to breathe
life into community
into friends who call

text, and visit
host dinner parties
and sleepovers
game nights
as the rest mourn
for the ghost that I was
and the ghost that
I have never actually been

In Reverse

they stare back
in reverse
a star fold
all major arcana
all reversed
the eyes of sabr
stares at me
knowing that patience
has never been
my virtue
the Minara
the Nafs
hold me
telling me that I
have used transformation
and self discovery
my tools
they are in reverse
broken like me
Sitara calls me
as the solstice begins
the Shams claims
my future like
it always has
also in reverse
Qamar beats into
my heart and very being
these cards are me
but broken
I am

my ilah pretends
it's greater than
the entire universe
as if we are not

one and the same
what am I holding
onto? That hurts me
again and again
why am I the one hurt?
again and again

Shams tells me
I am blocking its
light where it
is meant to be
my Joy hidden
unreachable
where is my Joy?
I finally cry
watching modern love
on the solstice

I translated Sabr
as patience, not temperance
I now wonder
if patience has
always been
about balance
I have known
the imbalance within me
but I can not tell you
why
it is in my depth
so much fire and ocean
earthquakes underneath
rumbling and a
sky I have lived in
endlessly
it is not a lack
an abundance
too much for me
to balance

I am resisting
my life is in upheaval
and I resist
somehow
what am I resisting?
is it saying no?
is it truth?
I lie all the time
to try to feel
safe
seen
valid
everything is a facade
is that what I resist?
truth only hurts
I am tired of
hurts

I'd translate
Sitara as veil
between worlds
boundaries
yet here it is star
perhaps the stars
are the lights to the curtains
or are the fabric
I am disconnected
from spirituality
burned out
not entirely sure
why
but I know
I know

what happens if
I empty my heart
to allow the moons
clarity into my soul

my heart feels
like an abyss
filled with holes and
crevices where everyone
is held hostage
then slips out
leaving scars from
their sharp sides

I am

I disassociate
colors blend and bleed
into nothing
ness

they call me
fig and I feel empty
I dance between
spaces, the lines
there and not there
a spirit of temper
ance

I send
love and appreciation
across the globe
impacting one thing
another
again and again
tears tightly held in
side

they call to
me, waving and
swaying in the light
breeze, their vibrance
hypnotizing and I
exhale, feel the fire to my
side and I rise
into the center of every
thing

I fly
allowing the sun
to ignite my

spiritual melanin
that abandons me during
winter here
glowing

                              i am

every
where

they ask me
if I like Emily in
Paris so far, between
medical emergencies
returning headphones and
responding to stray emails
I lie and say I like it
not a lie if I step back from
my rage against white
ness

I rage
spiritually and in every
existence but the solar
system does not need
two of us, two sun's
so I try to be
the moon but the ocean yearns
for home and I am not its home
like it is mine so I drift endlessly

they call me
High Priestess and
The Tower in tarot,
somedays,
I feel like the 9 or 10
of swords
despised chaos like
everything else within

I go home
to stars and suns and moons
I crave home, the tears of
the ocean
I crave my tears
on a solstice that echoes
beyond me to vaster
universes and planes to
morrow

So Close So far

my heart didn't ache
the days you were
in the ICU and no one told me
90 minutes away, a text or a call
would've reached me

had you still been my sister
I would have felt it in my bones
in our new state of friendship
I only carry my pain
pulmonary embolism and a blockage
in your lower intestines
you're at the wrong hospital
they talk to your mom about preparing
for death
we do not know where your advanced directive
lives

I am still 90 minutes away
I worry you will die with me so close
yet so far
I don't trust anyone would tell me to
come say goodbye
I am only an unpaid caretaker to them
you will die one day
I wonder if they'll tell me before
I feel it in my bones

Mourn

I feel you
slipping away
between time and space
your domains for eternity
your body lost
in this world and
maybe countless others
your soul transcending beyond
I will always be able to
visit with you
I know this
I do not mourn your physical body
in this realm
I mourn the shadows of what are
and could have been
I mourn the me that embraces
you, you are endless and
I have endless space to hold
you, I do

Mala for Caretaking

quartz, super 7 amethyst, dumortierite, rhodonite, calcite, carnelian obsidian, sandlewood, lava

quartz, fluorite, aquamarine, unicite jasper, golden rutilated quartz, carnelian, lava, sandalwood

quartz, super 7 amethyst, aquamarine, African turquoise, tigers eye, carnelian, black onyx

quartz, chevron amethyst, aquamarine, chrysocolla yellow calcite, carnelian, smokey quartz

quartz, fluorite, dumortierite, Burmese jade, calcite, carnelian, mahogany obsidian

smokey quartz, serpentine

Panic Attacks

panic attacks
my body too broken
for the 23 hours of
flights
praying to Allah
to open the skies
let me have an aisle
or window
I know it doesn't matter to
anyone else
I beg anyways
cry inside
so deep inside
death in the air
so many emotions

stage 3 kidney failure
stage 4 cancer
neck spasms
so much death
CBN gummy
falling asleep
delayed flight
will I melt into
this seat and disappear?

I'd like to...

200

it feels like S
will die when I reach 200
as if her life was
held at gunpoint by the
poetry her cancer inspired
the poetry her cancer demanded
of me, and now
it kills her when the cancer
couldn't

Bends and Always Breaks

it has been two weeks
since I saw you in the ICU
you are fine - I am not

my fractured mind bends and
breaks as your body heals
and regenerates

our souls are tied
it appears so is our healing

I will see a PT and a
Bipoc trans therapist
an MRI, some acupuncture
and hopefully carry yoga
in my soul

What Is and What Will Be

I let go
of you, of me
of the universe and everything
in between, as I yearn to just
be

yoga is more or less
the same as my own
Islamic and Palestinian
spiritual practice

with words not drowned in
the Tigris like ours were
words not villainized and defamed
it saddens, no
it just is the case
that some practices are villainized
though are the same

belief is a funny thing
when you pretend like
it was ever only
yours

today, I am,
what is meant to
happen will and everything else
won't

I float down
the Hanging Person (Tarot)
careless of name, gender
orientation

I am not this body

I am not this mind
we say in meditation and for the first time
claim both

at first I feel guilty
for this body-minds end
my mind tells me they are
not me, either

they are gifts to me
from countless others
who have also gone back
into the ground

I am not
them and they are not
me
we are partners for now

she calls me Yaffa
A..
S...
YAS I'm home

the wheel of time
turns and turns
lost sisters come
home

absences are and
are not
I am and
am not

one day you will
die
one day I will
too

we are
endless

Again

on a Sunday afternoon
3 months later
the sun shining on the east bay
first time since I've been back
the keys to the place I am moving into
in my hand, you say
I feel it, to the right of the one we mourned
a new tumor
stage 4, again
again
again

Beyond

July 2025

The Girl

I will always
come back
to you
to every version
I knew

the blind girl
making pottery

the girl who
befriended a black dog
that looked a lot
like the ones
who chased us
for sport

the girl who
sang, as if death
made you so much
more than the rest
of us

the girl who
knew I had no
stuffed animals
bought me my first

the girl who
inspired poetry
as I failed to hold
it all in

the girl who
spoke of magic
gemstones

protection spells

the girl who
couldn't honor
that I really needed
indigenous day of mourning
away from YT settlers

the girl who
texts
"sorry I didn't respond, I was in a coma"

the girl who
refused to communicate

the girl with
the shared stuffed
animals

the girl who
needed me
like the world
needed me
and after
25 years
I chose the
world
and you
died

the longest
story of death
in my world
most don't last
27 years
around me

Guests

your death
feels more real
as the bay
rises to intercept
my plane
we shake and wobble
as if we're not
welcome here
anymore
guests that overstay
their host

I want
to feel comfortable
enough with
someone
to cry
I want
someone to look
at me
know that I pretend
nothing impacts me
because if I
acknowledge my
sister is dead
then I won't be able
to breathe
who will breathe
for me
then?

I want
someone to hold me
witness all I am
know I can

witness them
too

how is it
that I have all
these loved ones
but no one
to talk to
about
you?

Yawn

I couldn't remember
your address
found you on
a map of pieces
of me left
behind

your garden
looks the same
bells ring
as if
waiting for you
to answer the door
bird feeder
empty
I wonder if
anyone has filled
it since I have
two years
ago

I feel the tears
but they don't come
instead it's my chest
tightening, breath lost
I want it out
like a yawn
but it won't
it won't
so I have a panic
attack
not sure what the panic
is for
or where is the
attack

Cry

finally
I cry
cry Cry like I've
never cried before

for the first time
cry for me
for the life I've
lived
all the harm
all the pain
all that I am

I drool, snot spilling
and I cry
it feels like
laughing
detoured on
its way out

I wish
someone could witness
me
hold me
there's just Me

I miss you
I miss me

good
bye

I feel
lighter
I am

light
it's uncontrollable
I am grateful
I cry
I have been
pretending to be
okay my entire life
have I ever been?

never cried in front of
anyone before
not even myself
I cried for me
not sure
if that's happened
before or will
ever again

I notice my
anxiety, avoiding messages
avoiding my people
wondering who is dead now
two years of genocide
your death on top
I'm terrified of who is leaving next
wondering if there's anyone
left to grieve
me

Epilogue

Nov 2025

It's the day of your memorial, four months later. An invite sits in my inbox from your best friend whose flight was canceled and could not be there. I am not there, I'm not sure where I am right now. I sit in a living room that's supposedly mine, yet dead plants sprinkled in the corners say otherwise.

I couldn't go. I couldn't take a single bus, an 18 minute journey to your old house. I couldn't see your loved ones and pretend as if they're also my loved ones. I couldn't forgive them for not telling me when you were in a coma. I don't forgive that none of them would have called me when you died if it wasn't for G. I give grace and resentment in equal measures and I can not go to another place where I do not feel safe to make others feel safe.

I have given whiteness 33 years of safety, I refuse to give a single ounce more. I will see your partner in the future and if our paths cross I will see your mom. I will definitely see G to mourn not just you but the thousands of hours of labor that is unrecognized. I was never your unpaid caretaker, I was your sibling.

You are the person I called sister more than any other, perhaps more than the seven biological sisters combined. I felt loved by you in a way that I was never loved by blood. Yet some days I wonder if we shared any love at all. I am sorry that we shared this timeline where it's impossible to know.

I grieve alone through this collection. You have not been in my life for two and a half years, and I potentially was never in yours except for as a caretaker. I grieve the sister I held in my heart, the sister I held in my arms as she died a thousand times, the sister I left behind. Perhaps I died first and you never made it into this new life. We have met in countless lifetimes but perhaps this was our last. May it be our last, may you finally rest.

I grieve through panic attacks wondering what is right, and like always I write to better understand myself and wonder if I'll find myself in these words.

No one asks if I'm okay today and I look at my life and wonder if maybe I'll never be treated any better than you treated me. I wonder how much caretaking I've done to build my karma so others take care of me. I wonder if I have ever cared at all. My friend reminds me that it's okay to hold both, that I do care and that it is an injustice to be treated the way I have when I have cared.

I do an EMDR session, trying to make sense of why I don't feel lovable unless I care for others and I wonder how much of that you've claimed. I hold the dual reality that you taught me acceptance and also at the same time taught me that I am unlovable. I wonder about your intentions and the cruelty of a world that would make you if your intentions were cruel. I do not fault you, I do not blame you, but I mourn the parts of us that could have existed in another world — the parts that existed in another world.

I mourn you as all that you were — imperfectly human. I mourn that at the very least you were a full family arc, one of love, of conflict, of care, of resentment, of immense love — something I do not have with my biological family.

I get up and pull out the tarot deck you gifted me — my very first. I ask for cards to allow me to honor you and me. A ten of wands, a reversed ten of swords, and a reversed strength. Our journey is over, on the path to recovery, but I will stumble first.

I would love to end these words with the most loving of endings, but love, family, and cancer do not always end with a bowtied ending. There is healing today, yesterday, and everyday moving forward, but like the journey it is messy, bloody, and filled with uncertainty. We do it anyway. I would go on this journey with you again and again. The ending has never mattered. We lived instead. There's no better way that I know to honor you than to honor that reality.

I love you, may you always be at rest.

Your sibling,
Legal Name held hostage by the hospitals we lived in

Acknowledgements

Thank you to everyone who stood by me through this journey, the before, during, and after. Thank you to Genevieve specifically for the support!

Thank you to Michael Colgan for being the first to witness these poems and offer thoughts and suggestions.

Thank you to Andrea Ramos Campos for helping bring this work to life.

Thank you to Mishandi Sarhan for the beautiful cover design and capturing the essence of this poetry collection. Sassy and I's journey was filled with tea and conversation, chai was a staple.

Thank you to the plants that play such a pivotal role in my life. Thistle captures so much of this journey and is the national flower of Scotland, where my sister's ancestors are from.

About Yaffa

Mx. Yaffa is an author and storyteller that paves the way for us to imagine utopia through every word. Yaffa's poetry, non-fiction, and speculative fiction books have been sold globally and translated to various languages.

Mx. Yaffa is an acclaimed disabled, autistic, trans, queer, Muslim, and indigenous Palestinian individual who has received multiple awards for their transformative work around displacement, decolonization, equity, and centering the lived experiences of individuals most impacted by injustice.

About Meraj Publishing

Meraj Publishing is a Disabled Trans Palestinian Muslim owned rapid response publishing house that centers Trans global majority voices impacted by genocide. Recognizing the vast inequities in the publishing industry and the often long processes to have a work published. Meraj aims to publish writing by individuals most impacted as soon as possible to inform the on the ground organizing and world building needs. Meraj prioritizes stories that focus on organizing, world building, building utopia, hope, love, spirituality, and belonging. Meraj Publishing is entirely run and operated by Trans and Queer global majority individuals.

www.ingramcontent.com/pod-product-compliance
Lightning Source LLC
Chambersburg PA
CBHW070546090426
42735CB00013B/3085